A COMPLETE USER GUIDE TO IPAD PRO 2020

A step by step guide to your iPad pro 11 or 12.9 inches

Bernard Gates

Introduction 10

Chapter one: set up 11

Setting up your iPad pro as New... 11

Transferring your stuff from a Current iPad to your new iPad pro.... 12

Moving your Data to your New iPad pro via your Mac.................. 14

Transferring your stuff to your new iPad pro via iCloud 16

Chapter 2: cellular and Wi-Fi connections.. 18

To use an eSIM: 18

To use a nano SIM: 19

Connecting your iPad pro to a Cellular Network 19

Changing your cellular Plan 20

Deactivating your cellular Data Plan 20

Moving your Data Plan from your old Device to New 20

Using Wi-Fi for Data Connectivity 20

Chapter 3: FaceID 22

Setting up Face ID.. 22

Turning off Required Attention for Face ID 23

Turning on Attention Awareness for Face ID................................. 24

Adding a Second Face to Face ID 24

Chapter 4: Apple Pay 25

Adding a card to Apple Pay 25

Changing the default Card for Apple Pay 27

Removing a Card from Apple Pay 27

Changing information and Card Settings for a Card 27

Chapter 5: Siri 28

Turning on Siri 28

Training Siri with your voice 28

Using "Hey Siri" 29

Using AirPods or EarPods with Siri 29

Using AirPods or EarPods to Listen to and Respond to Messages... 29

Chapter 6: Basic functions of iPad..................................**31**

Wake and sleep your iPad pro.................................... 31

Volume controls 31

Changing Sounds for Notifications and Alerts 32

Locating Settings 33

Changing screen Brightness and Color........................ 33

Adjusting Screen Brightness Automatically 33

Turning dark Mode on and off 33

Setting Dark Mode to Turn on and off Automatically 34

Changing your iPad pro Name 35

Setting the Date and Time... 35

Setting Language and Region 36

Accessing Features and Information from the Lock Screen 38

Screen shots and Screen Recording 38

Changing the Default WallPaper.................................. 39

Searching with iPad 39

performing Quick Actions 40

Chapter 7: mail and Contacts **41**

Setting up a Mail Account 41

Setting up a Contacts Account..................................... 42

Chapter 8: Using Apps on iPad **43**

Using the Dock to open an App 43

Accessing Apps from the App Switcher 43

Organizing Your Apps into the Dock or other Locations 43

Organizing your Apps in Folders 44

Resetting Apps to original Positions... 44

Deleting Apps and Folders 44

Closing an App.. 44

Using Two Apps in Split View 44

Using Slide Over to open and view Apps 45

Changing Apps being viewed in Slide Over 45

Using picture in picture on iPad pro to Multi-Task 45

Using Drag and Drop to Move Items 46

Moving or Copying an item between Apps in Split Screen or Slide
Over 46

Copying an item to an app on the Home Screen or in the Dock 47

Dragging and Dropping Multiple items 47

Chapter 9: keyboard, Text and Typing **48**

Using the Onscreen Keyboard 48

Using the Onscreen Keyboard as a Trackpad 48

using Accented Letters While Typing 48

Using Predictive Text and Auto Correction............................. 49

Using the dictating Function of iPad 49

Selecting and Editing Text.. 49

Inserting Text Via Typing 50

Adding or Removing a Keyboard 50

Changing to Another Keyboard 51

Chapter 10: AirDropping Items **52**

Using AirDrop to send an item.. 52

Receiving items via AirDrop 52

Chapter 11: Mark up **53**

Drawing or Writing in markup supported Apps....................... 53

Drawing a Shape 53

Showing, Hiding and Moving the Toolbar................................. 53

Adding Typed Text and Shapes... 54

Erasing an Error... 54

Adding and Adjusting shapes in Supported Apps...................... 54

Adding your Signature.. 55

Chapter 12: Control Center... 56

Opening and Closing Control Center 56

Accessing More Controls from Control Center 56

Adding and Organizing Controls... 56

Deactivating Access to Control Center in Apps 57

Chapter 13: Notifications and Do not Disturb........................ 58

Accessing your Notifications... 58

Responding to Notifications 58

Other Options 58

Changing Notifications Settings 59

Showing Recent Notifications on the Lock Screen..................... 59

Silencing All Notifications/Activating Do Not Disturb................ 59

Allowing Calls with Do Not Disturb Activated......................... 59

Allowing Emergency Contacts Calls with Do Not Disturb 59

Chapter 14: widgets 61

Today view 61

Today View widgets on your Home screen 61

Adding widgets from the widget gallery................................. 61

Repositioning or removing widgets 62

Customizing a Widget.. 62

Removing Today View from your Home screen 62

Allowing Access to Today View if iPad pro is Locked 62

Chapter 15: iOS 14 features 63

Getting App Clips 63

Using your iPad proto Make and Receive Calls 63

Using scribble on iPad 64

Entering Text with Apple Pencil from any Text Field 64

Entering Text with Apple Pencil in Notes 64

Using Apple Pencil to Highlight and make Changes to Text 65

Using the Notes Function to Draw or Write 65

Selecting and Editing Drawings and Handwriting 66

Guides Feature of Maps App 66

Cycling Directions from current Maps Location 67

Chapter 16: using iPad pro to control home accessories 69

Adding an Accessory to Home on your iPad 69

Changing an Accessory's Location Assignment 69

Using Control Center to control Accessories 70

Editing Home Accessories 71

Grouping and controlling Accessories 71

Viewing your Home status 71

Setting up and using Face Recognition 72

Using Face Recognition to identify Visitors and Add them to your
Photo Library 73

Receiving Notifications from Camera or Doorbells 73

Enabling others to view Faces in your Library 73

Organizing Rooms or Parts of your House into Zones 73

Editing a Room 74

Chapter 17: sending messages on iPad 75

Sending a Message 75

Reply to a Message...75

Replying to a Specific Message in a Conversation.............................75

Pinning and Unpinning a Conversation 76

Switching from a Messages Conversation to a FaceTime or Audio Call
....76

Copying a contact in conversations...76

Changing a group name and photo 76

Using Business Chat...76

Sending Memoji and Memoji Stickers 77

Creating your very own Memoji..77

Chapter 18: camera, video and photos................................ 78

Taking a Photo 78

Taking a panoramic shot 79

Taking a selfie..80

Taking and viewing burst shots 80

Taking and viewing live photos..81

Recording a Video 81

Recording a Slow-motion Video..81

Capturing a Time-Lapse Video...81

Filtering photos in Albums 82

Using Folders to Organize Albums 82

Viewing Photos 82

Customizing and playing a Slideshow..83

Chapter 19: FaceTime 84

Making a FaceTime Call 84

Making a Group FaceTime Call 84

Starting a Group FaceTime call from a Group Messages Conversation
....85

Adding a New Participant to a Call 85

Exiting a Group FaceTime Call 85

Chapter 20: family sharing 86

Setting up Family Sharing 86

Adding a New Family Member 86

Setting up an Apple ID for a child 87

Viewing what you are sharing in your Family Group 88

Exiting or Deactivating Family Sharing 88

Downloading Shared Purchases from iTunes Store 88

Downloading shared purchases from App Store................................. 89

Downloading shared purchases from Apple Books 89

Downloading Shared Purchases from the Apple TV app 90

Deactivating purchase Sharing 90

Activating Ask to Buy For Children 90

Activating Apple Cash Family for a Child 90

Sharing Subscriptions and iCloud storage with family members 91

Setting Up your iPad pro to be Found 91

Sharing your Location with your Family Members 92

Chapter 21: using your iPad pro with other Apple Products 93

Using your iPad proas a Hotspot 93

Connecting other Apple Devices to your iPad pro Hotspot 94

Tethering your Mac or PC to your iPad pro Hotspot 94

Using your iPad pro to Make and Receive Calls 95

Making or Receiving a Call on Your iPad 96

Using iPad pro as a Dual Display for your Mac 96

Changing Sidecar Preferences 98

Handing off Tasks between Your iPad pro and Mac........................... 98

Deactivating Handoff on your Devices 99

Using the universal clipboard function to Cut, Copy and Paste between your Devices 100

Syncing your Mac or PC with your iPad 100

Syncing Between your Windows PC and iPad 101

Using Wi-Fi Syncing 101

Moving files between your iPad pro and Mac or PC 101

Moving Files Between your iPad pro and PC 102

Chapter 22: Troubleshooting **103**

Shutting down and restarting iPad 103

Doing a Hard Restart 104

Updating your iPad pro OS 104

Backing up your iPad 104

Returning your iPad pro Settings to factory Settings 105

Wiping your iPad pro contents 105

Wiping your iPad pro via a Computer 105

Introduction

The iPad pro to put it simply, is the most advanced and up to date iteration of the Apple iPad proline up. Its accurate to say that you could pass up buying a laptop computer and buy this device instead. It can do almost everything a full laptop is capable and even better

The iPad pro 2020 comes in two sizes. It can be purchased in an 11- or 12.9-inches package. Whichever one it is, it has an all screen design and edge to edge display and does not feature a Home button.

Talking about the features, the pro model is bristling with a number of functions such as smart HDR, True Tone flash, TrueDepth camera system, LIDAR, dual rear cameras, liquid retina display, pro motion, 4k video recording, 5 studio quality microphones, 4 speakers etc.

Under the hood, the pro model has the A12z Bionic chip processor with an 8 core GPU and 8 core CPU, 6GB ram, a neural engine and enhanced thermal architecture. There's even tuned performance controllers for blistering fast response and output. The cameras include a 12mega pixel wide angle camera and a 10 mega pixel ultra-wide-angle camera.

For connectivity, the pro model has a USB-C port for linking with accessories that use such connection and for a charging purpose for both the iPad pro and other Apple devices like your iPhone and Apple watch. Other accessories include the Apple pencil 2nd generation which could also be charged via a magnetic connection and the magic keyboard. The pro also comes with Wi-Fi 6 support as standard and gigabit class LTE for cellular versions.

The iPad pro is ideal for media consumption, browsing, apps and productivity. The battery can stay up to 10 hours

The iPad pro 2020 can be had in two finishes: silver space grey aluminum and starts from $799 for the 11-inch 128GB Wi-Fi model or $949 for the 128GB cellular model. The 12.9-inch version starts from $999 for 128GB Wi-Fi model and $1,149 for the 128GB cellular model. You can get additional storage but have to pay a lot more.

Chapter one: set up

There are 3 ways of setting up your iPad: as new, from an Apple device backup or from another device. If you purchased your iPad pro new, take the following steps

Setting up your iPad pro as New

- Power on the iPad. (you may decide to fully charge it before powering it on) You should see the Apple logo

Top button

- Slide to set up by swiping your finger across the screen
- Select a **language**
- Select a **region or country**
- From the Quick start screen, you have the option of using an existing iPhone or iPad proto continue the set up or you can tap **Set Up Manually**
- Select a **Wi-Fi network** and enter the passcode or tap **Use Cellular** if you have a data version iPad
- Click **Continue** on the Data & Privacy screen
- Next you set up the **FaceID**. If you decide to set up later, tap **Set Up FaceID Later**. If you decide to set it up immediately, click **Get Started**
- Next, set up a **passcode**. Unlike in iOS13, you don't have the option of skipping this step. iOS14 is set up to mandatorily require a passcode.
- From the **Apps & Data** screen, select from the options how to transfer apps and data to your iPad. If you elect not to do a transfer, tap **Don't Transfer Data & Apps**
- Next log into **Apple ID**. If you can't remember your ID or don't have **one, tap Forgot password or Don't Have an Apple ID?** and follow the instructions

- On the **Express Settings** screen, tap continue if you prefer not to adjust the settings or tap **Customize Settings** if you want to
- On the next screen, tap **Continue** to keep your iPad pro up to date
- Next set up **Apple Pay** or do it later from **Settings.**
- Tap **Continue** if you want to allow the iCloud Keychain to save your credit cards and passwords information
- Click continue to set up **Siri** or do it later from **Settings**
- Enable **Screen Time** if you want to keep track of your usage by tapping **Continue** or tap **Turn on Later in Settings**
- Choose an option from the **App Analytics** screen or tap **Don't Share** if you don't want to
- On the **Appearance** screen, choose between **Light** or **Dark** mode and tap **Continue**
- You will now see a **Welcome to iPad** message. Tap **Get Started**

Transferring your stuff from a Current iPad to your new iPad pro
You need iOS 11 or later to do this

- Begin the set-up process as outlined above
- Select a **Language**
- Tap **Continue** when asked to set up your new iPad pro with your **Apple ID**

- Scan the image that appears with your old iPad

- Key in the **passcode** to your old iPad on the new one you are setting up
- Set up **Touch ID**

- Decide if you want to restore your new device from your latest compatible backup
- Decide if you want to restore your new iPad pro from iCloud or iTunes, set it up as new or move data from an old device

- Next, **Agree** to the terms and conditions
- From **Express settings**, tap **Continue** to use the settings for Siri, Find My iPhone, Location, and usage analytics moved over from your previous device

Settings from your iPhone

- Finish up the set-up process

Moving your Data to your New iPad pro via your Mac
- Connect your old device to your Mac
- Select **Finder** from the Dock to launch a new Finder Window
- Select the **iPad pro** from the side bar

- Tick the **checkbox** next to **Encrypt local backup** if you decide want an encryption
- Key in a password if you select to encrypt backups

 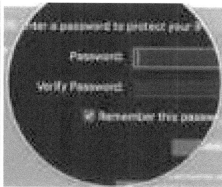

- On the next display, Select **Back Up Now.** When it's done, disconnect the iPad

- Next, connect the new **iPad pro**to the Mac
- Select the new **iPad pro** from the **side bar**
- Click the button next to **Restore from this backup**

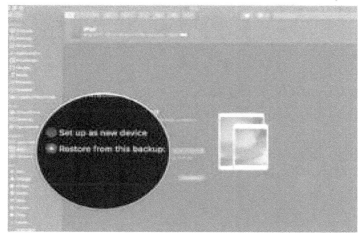

- Select a **backup** from the dropdown bar
- Select **Continue**

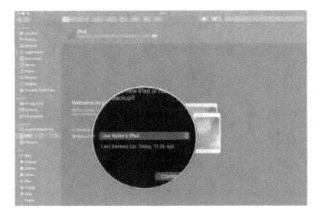

- Next, obey the instructions on your new iPad proto complete the setup

Transferring your stuff to your new iPad pro via iCloud

Before doing this, make sure you do a back up to ensure that what you will move to your new iPad pro is as up to date as possible

- Launch **Settings** on your old device
- Tap **Apple ID**. Tap **iCloud**

- Tap **iCloud Backup**. Tap **Back Up Now**

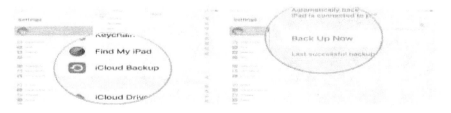

When you are done with the backup on your old iPad, the next step is to move the back up to your new device. follow the steps below

- Push top button on the **new iPad pro** and follow the initial set up instructions
- Next tap **Restore from [date of most recent backup] Back up** to restore your new iPad pro with the most recent saved back up when you are using Automatic Setup
- Next tap **Agree**

- Complete the setup on your new iPad pro with settings for Siri, Location, app analytics and Apple Pay
- The new iPad pro will now restore via the iCloud backup. This process may take a little time.

Chapter 2: cellular and Wi-Fi connections

If you purchased an iPad pro with both cellular and Wi-Fi connections, you have the flexibility of alternating between both connections when you have to.

You have 3 options. You could use an eSIM, an embedded Apple SIM or a third-party nano SIM from a cellular provider.

To use an eSIM:
- Launch **Setting**s.
- Tap **Cellular Data**
- Next, choose a **carrier** and follow the onscreen instructions
- If you want to add another plan, tap **Add a New Plan**
- If you have to scan a QR code, from **Settings**, turn on **Mobile Data.**
- Next, place the iPad pro in such a way that your carrier's QR code appears in the frame. You can also choose to enter the details manually. You may be asked for a carrier provided confirmation code.

- In case you have more than one eSIM setup on your device, bear in mind, you can use just one at a time. If you want to switch between eSIMs, follow the steps below:
1. Launch **Settings.**
2. Tap **Cellular Data.**
3. Tap **your preferred plan**

You have the option of setting up your cellular connection via your carrier's app if its available. All you need do is to download your carrier's app from the App store and use it to buy a plan.

To use a nano SIM:
- Use a sim tray ejector pin to make the tray open by placing the pin in the tiny hole on the outer part of the tray and pushing inwards

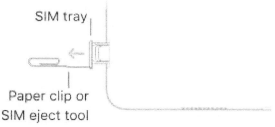

SIM tray

Paper clip or
SIM eject tool

- Bring out the **tray** from the iPad
- Next, place the **nano-SIM** correctly in the **SIM tray** as shown below

Nano-SIM

- Put the **sim tray** back in correctly
- Key in the PIN if you have it activated on the SIM

Connecting your iPad pro to a Cellular Network
If you have setup a SIM card on your device, do the following:

- Go to **Settings.**
- Turn on **Cellular or Mobile Data.**

Changing your cellular Plan

If you have several plans setup on your iPad, you can switch to any one by taking the following steps:

- Launch **Settings**. From **mobile Data**, select a plan under **Mobile Data Plans**

Deactivating your cellular Data Plan

There are two types of plans: pre-paid and post-paid. For a prepaid plan, when it runs out, don't renew it. For a post-paid plan, follow steps below:

- Launch **Settings.**
- Go to **Mobile Data**
- Tap **operator name** and select not to renew your plan

Moving your Data Plan from your old Device to New

For a SIM card mobile data plan:

- Shut down both devices
- Open the **SIM tray** on both devices using the specified tool
- Transfer the **SIM card** from the old iPad proto the new one and close both trays
- Power on both devices again and wait for the setup or activation process to finish
  For an eSIM:
    - Launch **Settings** on the new iPad.
    - Go to **Mobile Data.**
    - Go to **Set Up Mobile Data**
    - Tap the **Transfer button** next to your preferred service provider and obey the instructions to effect the transfer. If it's not there, contact your service provider

Using Wi-Fi for Data Connectivity

If during your set up of your iPad, you set up a Wi-Fi connection, all you need do is:

- Launch **Settings**.
- Turn on **Wi-Fi**. A connection should automatically be established if you have a saved network.
- If you have several networks or hotspots, or you want to switch to another, just tap on the **network or hotspot name** and key in the **password** if necessary

- If a connection is established, you should see a symbol at top right of the screen

Chapter 3: FaceID

Face ID is a security feature or function of certain Apple devices such as iPad and iPhone. The iPad pro is one such equipped device. Face ID is a biometric facial identity scanner that has a dual purpose of unlocking your iPad pro and authorizing purchases from App store, Apple pay, and iTunes. If you didn't set up and activate the Face ID function during the initial set up of your iPad pro, here's how you can do it below:

Setting up Face ID

- Launch **settings**
- Next, tap **Face ID & passcode**

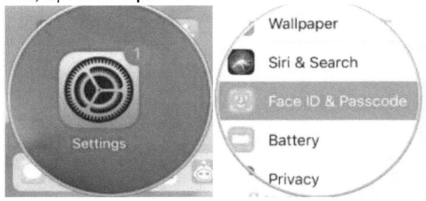

- Key in your **passcode**
- On the next display, **tap Set Up Face ID**

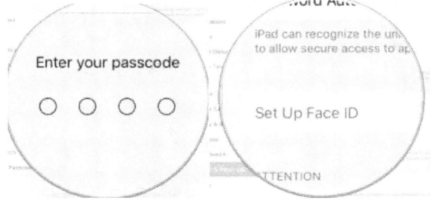

- Tap **Get Started**
- When you see the circle, position **your face** inside it

- Now, move **your head** slowly in a circle and tap **Continue**
- Next, you will be required to move **your head** slowly in a second circle
- Tap **Done**
- You can now use your face to unlock your iPad pro

Turning off Required Attention for Face ID

If you want to set up your iPad pro so you don't have to look directly at it for logins or purchase authentications, here's how:

- Follow steps 1-3 as above in setting up Face ID
- Next, switch the **Require Attention for Face ID** button to off

- Tap **Ok** to confirm

Turning on Attention Awareness for Face ID

If this is activated, the system would verify if you are looking at your screen before dimming the display or lowering the volume of alerts.

- Follow the first 3 steps as above in setting up Face ID
- Switch the **Attention Awareness Features** button to on

Adding a Second Face to Face ID

- Follow first 3 steps as in setting up Face ID
- Next tap Set Up an Alternate Appearance

- To complete the process, follow the steps used in Setting up Face ID

Chapter 4: Apple Pay

With Apple pay, you can make in-store and online purchases with your iPad. With a scan of your face, you get it done. It makes for more secure credit and debit card purchases.

Adding a card to Apple Pay

- From your home screen, launch the **Wallet** app
- Tap the **+ button** at top right corner of your screen.
- Tap **Continue** or **Next** on the Apple Pay screen.

- You can manually enter, or choose to scan with the camera, your **credit or debit card information**. For you to use the scan option, your card must have embossed numbers. If not, you have to use the manual option.
- Tap **Next**
- Manually enter the card's details such as **expiration date** and the **security code**.

- Tap **Next. Agree** to the terms and conditions. Tap **Agree**

- Select your verification method and tap **Next**
- Tap **Enter Code**.
- Key in the **verification code** you were given

- Tap **Next**
- Tap **Done**

Use these steps to add more cards if you want which could include cards you use with Apple pay on other devices.

Changing the default Card for Apple Pay

- Go to the **Settings app** on your iPad pro that's compatible with Apple Pay.

- Tap **Wallet & Apple Pay**.

- Tap **Default Card**.

- Tap on the **card** you want as your default.

Removing a Card from Apple Pay

- Go to the **Settings app**

- Tap **Wallet & Apple Pay**.

- Tap on the **credit card**

- Tap **Remove This Card**. Scroll down to screen bottom

Changing information and Card Settings for a Card

- Launch **Settings**.
- Tap **wallet & Apple pay**
- Tap a card.
- You can decide to see your history by tapping **Transactions.** You can see the last four digits of the card, change the billing address or delete the card from Apple Pay

Chapter 5: Siri

Siri is your personal assistant that helps you get things done as regards using your device to find out things and get information, making calls, sending messages etc. **Your device must have an internet connection for siri to work**

Turning on Siri

By default, during the initial setup of your iPad, you will be prompted to set Siri up and walked through the steps. If you elected to do so later, here's how you can do it:

- Launch **Settings**.
- Tap **Siri & Search.**
- Switch on **Listen for Hey Siri**
- To summon Siri with EarPods or AirPods, **press and hold the center or call button or press and hold the force sensor or double tap one of the AirPods**

Training Siri with your voice

You have to get siri to know your voice. Follow these steps:

- On the Set Up "Hey Siri" page, tap **Continue**

- Say, **"Hey Siri."**

- Next, say, **"Hey Siri, Send a Message**

- say, **"Hey Siri, How's the Weather Today?"**

- say, **"Hey Siri, set a timer for three minutes."**

- say, **"Hey Siri, play some music."**

- Tap **Done** on the **"Hey Siri" Is Ready page**

- To retrain Siri with your voice: from **Settings,** turn off and turn on Listen for "Hey Siri" and repeat the voice training steps

Using "Hey Siri"

- Place yourself close enough to your iPad

- Say "Hey Siri!" loud enough for your iPad proto hear

- Let Siri know what you want it to do — "call my wife on speaker", "make a movie reservation", "what's the weather like in Australia?", etc.

- To ask Siri something else or give a different task, tap the Siri icon .

- If you have to rephrase your request, tap the **Siri icon** and then say your request differently

- You may have to sometimes spell out part of your request if need be. For e.g, if siri doesn't understand the task or a part of it. Tap the **Siri icon** and do the spelling

- If you want to change a message just before sending it, say **"change it"**

- If you want to edit your request via text, when you see it on the screen, **tap on it** and use the **onscreen keyboard** to edit

- If you prefer to type your instructions or requests, summon Siri and use the keyboard to interact with Siri. To turn this function on: launch **Settings**, tap **Accessibility**, tap **Siri** and switch on **Type to Siri**

Using AirPods or EarPods with Siri

Make sure you have activated Siri and you have an internet connection. Your AirPods or EarPods must also be paired with your iPad.

- Using AirPods or EarPods with Siri is much the same as outlined above under Using "Hey Siri": say **"Hey Siri"** and give ask your question or make a request

Using AirPods or EarPods to Listen to and Respond to Messages

You have to turn on Announce Messages when pairing your AirPods with your iPad. Do it thus:

- launch **Settings.**
- Go to **Siri & Search.**
- Tap **Announce Messages.** Switch on **Announce Messages with Siri**
- When a get a message, you hear a chime and Siri reads it.
- If you want to respond to the message, say something like: "Reply ok that's fine"
- To stop Siri from reading you can:
  1. Say Something like**: "Stop" or "Cancel"**
  2. **Remove an AirPod**
  3. **Press the force sensor** on any of your AirPods pro or **double-tap any of your AirPods** (2nd generation)
- Siri is setup to confirm your instruction by repeating it before sending. To send without Siri's confirmation, do the following**:**
  1. launch **Settings,**
  2. go to **Siri & Search.**
  3. Tap **Announce Messages**
  4. Turn on **Reply Without Confirmation**

Chapter 6: Basic functions of iPad

There are basic features and functions of your that you need to get accustomed to so that you can get familiarized with how it works. Find them below.

Wake and sleep your iPad pro

There are 4 ways you can use to wake your iPad.

- You can wake it by pressing the **top button** as shown below:

- You can also use your **Apple Pencil** to wake the iPad pro by **tapping the screen**

Using Face ID to Unlock iPad pro

- If you have FaceID set up, to wake your iPad pro is as easy as using your face to unlock the iPad

Using a passcode to unlock iPad

- If you set up your iPad pro to require a passcode, just press the **top button** and enter the **passcode**
- To lock your iPad, just press the **top button**. Your iPad pro would also go to sleep automatically after a set period of time

Volume controls

The volume buttons are situated on the right side of the iPad

Volume buttons

- To increase the volume, press the **top button.**
- To reduce the volume, press the **lower button**
- To use **Siri,** you can say "Turn up the volume or Turn down the Volume
- If you want to mute the sounds, press and hold the **volume down button**
- To adjust the volume from **control Center**, launch the **Control Center** and drag the **volume icon** ◀)).
- To silence the sounds for some time**, launch Control Center** and tap the 🌙 Do not Disturb icon.
- To set a volume limit for headphones,
    1. launch **Settings,**
    2. tap **Sounds,**
    3. tap **Reduce Loud Sounds,**
    4. switch on **Reduce Loud Sounds**
    5. **drag the slider** to select maximum level

Changing Sounds for Notifications and Alerts
If you don't like the default sounds for incoming messages and alerts, you can change it.

- Launch **Settings.**
- Tap **Sounds.**
- Tap **Ringtone** and other Options to choose or set your preferred sounds like Text Tone, New Mail, Sent Mail, Calendar Alerts, Reminder Alerts and AirDrop

Locating Settings

You can use the **Settings app** to adjust or change settings on your iPad.

- To access **Settings**, tap it on your **Home Screen**. It looks like a wheel inside a gray square

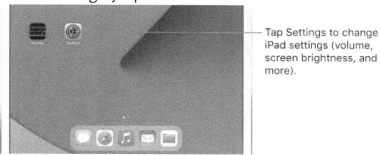

Tap Settings to change iPad settings (volume, screen brightness, and more).

Changing screen Brightness and Color

- Launch **Settings**.
- Tap **Display & Brightness**. Use the slider to increase or decrease the brightness
- You can also go to **Control Center** and then drag the brightness icon ☀

Adjusting Screen Brightness Automatically

- Launch **Settings**.
- Tap **Accessibility**
- Tap **Display & Text Size** and activate **Auto-Brightness**

Turning dark Mode on and off

- Launch Settings.
- Tap **Display & Brightness**
- Choose **Dark** to turn it on or **Light** to turn it off

Setting Dark Mode to Turn on and off Automatically

- Launch **Settings.**
- Turn on **Display and Brightness.**

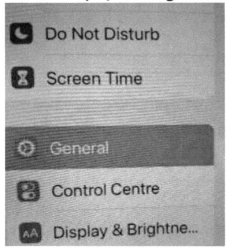

- Switch on **Automatic** and tap **Options**
- Choose between **Sunset to Sunrise** or **Custom Schedule**
- If you opt for **Custom Schedule,** you have to set the times you want **Dark Mode** to work

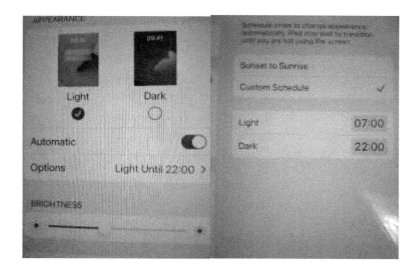

Changing your iPad pro Name

- Launch **Settings**
- Tap **General**
- Tap **About**
- Tap **Name**
- Tap **X** and enter the name you want and tap **Done**

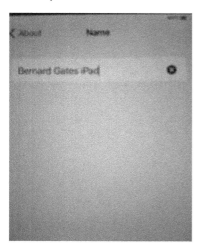

Setting the Date and Time

- Launch **Settings**
- Tap **General**
- Tap **Date & Time**

- You can select **Set Automatically** but if you prefer to set the time yourself, switch off **Set Automatically** and set date and time to your preference

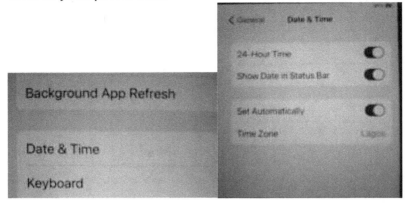

Setting Language and Region

If you didn't do this during initial set up or you want to alter the settings, follow the steps below:

- Launch **Settings**.
- Tap **General.**
- Tap **Language & Region**

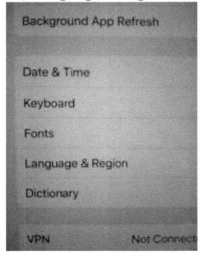

- From this display, you can set **language, region, calendar format and temperature**

If your language is not English or you want to add a keyboard for another language, do the following:

- Launch **Settings**
- Tap **General**
- Tap **Keyboards**
- Tap **Add New Keyboard**

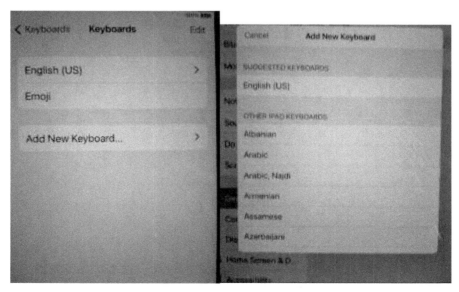

- Select your preferred **keyboard** from List

Accessing Features and Information from the Lock Screen

There are basic functions that you can quickly access from the lock screen. Find them as follows:

- To launch the Camera, **swipe left** from the lock screen
- To view previous notifications, **swipe upwards** from the center from the lock screen
- To access Today view, **swipe right** from the lock screen
- To launch Control Center, **swipe down** from top-right of the screen
- To draw and take notes using Apple Pencil, **tap the Pencil** on the lock screen

Screen shots and Screen Recording

If you see something on your screen you want to save as a picture or record to share with others, here's what you can do:

- press and release the **top and volume button** at the same time
- next, tap the **screenshot** at lower left and tap **Done**
- select where to save the screenshot

To do a Screen Recording, follow the steps below:
- launch **Settings.**
- Tap **Control Center.**

- Next, Tap the green circle with a white cross inside it next to Screen Recording

- Launch **control Center.** Tap ⬤ and wait for the countdown before the recording starts

- Use the ⊙ button or icon to stop the recording and tap **Stop**

Changing the Default WallPaper

If you don't like the wallpaper on your iPad, you can change it by taking a picture and setting it as your wallpaper. You can also select a picture from your gallery.

- Launch **Settings.**
- Tap **Wallpaper.**
- Tap **Choose a New Wallpaper.**
- You can choose a picture from the default images or select from your own pictures
- **Pinch open to zoom** in on the picture and **pinch closed** to return to normal appearance as you set it according to your preference

Searching with iPad

- To choose which items to search from, launch **Settings**, tap **Siri & Search**, navigate down, tap an app and turn **Show in Search** on or off
- To search for apps, names, etc, **swipe down** from the middle of the **home screen,** tap the **search field** and enter what you want to locate
- You can tap **Go** to hide the keyboard and view more results
- You can tap a suggested app to open it
- to get more information about an app tap it and tap a result to open it

- if you want to search for something else tap ⊗ in the search field

- to search while in an app, tap the **search field** or the **magnifying glass icon.** You can swipe down from **screen top** if there is no search field. Type your search and tap **Search**

 performing Quick Actions

Quick actions are shortcuts you can use to quickly access options in an app, mail home screen or Control Center etc

- from **Mail, touch and hold a message** to view the contents and see your options
- for icons on the **Home screen, touch and hold an app icon** to open a menu
- in **photos, touch and hold an image** to view it and view options
- in the **Control Center, touch and hold an item** to view options
- from the lock screen, touch and hold a notification to respond to it
- **touch and hold the space bar with a finger** while typing if you want to turn the keyboard into a trackpad

Chapter 7: mail and Contacts

You can set up your mail using other popular internet-based mail in addition to the apps that are on your device. you can also set up contacts etc

Setting up a Mail Account

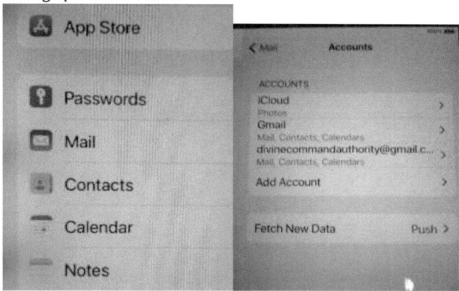

- Launch **Settings.**
- Tap **Mail.**
- Tap **Accounts.**
- Tap **Add Account**
- Tap an **email service** and enter your account information

- If your email provider is not included, tap **Other**, tap **Add Mail Account** and enter the required information

Setting up a Contacts Account
- Launch **Settings.**
- Tap **Contacts.**
- Tap **Accounts.**
- Tap **Add Account.**
- Tap **Other.**
- Tap Add LDAP Account or Add CardDAV Account and enter your server and account information

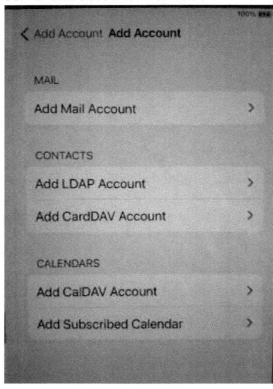

Chapter 8: Using Apps on iPad

Your iPad pro comes with some Apps by default. You can also download more Apps from the Apple App store. You can switch between apps and do a lot more.

There are 3 ways of opening or switching between Apps.

Using the Dock to open an App

- While you are in any app, **swipe up** from screen bottom. The dock should appear.
- Next, **tap the app** you want to use

Accessing Apps from the App Switcher

- **Swipe up** from screen bottom and then hold your finger in screen center. You can also tap the **Home button** twice in quick succession
- **Swipe to left and right** to view the open apps

Organizing Your Apps into the Dock or other Locations

- **Tap and hold** any app.
- Tap **Edit Home Screen**

- You can now move any app to the Dock at screen bottom, a new position on the same page or another Home Screen page.
- To move the app to a new Home Screen page, **move it to screen edge** and wait for the new page to show
- Tap **Done** at top right when you are done

Organizing your Apps in Folders
- Follow the first 2 steps as above
- When the apps jiggle, **drag an app onto another** to create a new folder
- To populate the folder, drag more apps into the folder
- Tap and hold the **name field** to change the folder name. you can also tap and hold the folder until a small sub screen appears
- Select **Rename** and tap **Done** from keyboard or tap anywhere on the screen when you are finished

Resetting Apps to original Positions
- Launch **Settings.** Tap **General.** Tap **Reset**
- Tap **Reset Home Screen Layout**

Deleting Apps and Folders
- To delete an app, **tap and hold the app** till the options sub screen appears. Tap **Delete App** at bottom
- To delete created folders, move all the apps out of it and its deleted.

Closing an App
- Open the **App Switcher** and swipe upwards on the app
- Tap the app on the Home Screen to reopen

Using Two Apps in Split View
- Open an app. While in the app, **swipe up** from bottom edge to show the Dock
- **Tap and hold the second app** you want to open. Move it to right or left edge of screen and remove your finger
- To replace a previously open app in split screen, just move the replacing app over the one you want to replace it with

- Use the **app divider** at the center in between both apps to share equal space between the apps
- To close the split view, **drag the divider to left or right of screen** based on the app you want to remove

Using Slide Over to open and view Apps

The slide over function allows apps to slide in front of one another so you can effectively multi-task as you use your iPad.

- From an open app, **swipe up** from bottom and wait to call up the **Dock**
- Tap and hold an app in the Dock and move it above the Dock
- Any open app will be replaced by the app you move from the Dock
- **Drag an app** from the Dock to the **split view divider** to launch a third app in slide over

Changing Apps being viewed in Slide Over

- To switch between apps, you have 3 options:
- You can **swipe up** from the bottom of the slide Over window, you can **tap on the app** you want to view if you can see it or you can **swipe right** through the apps

Using picture in picture on iPad pro to Multi-Task

Picture in picture basically allows you to use or view videos while using other apps.

- From FaceTime or a video, press the **Home Button**

- When the video window reduces to a part of your screen, you can view the **Home Screen** and launch other apps. You have some options available to you which are:
- **Pinch open** the small video window to increase its dimension and **pinch closed** to return to small size
- Tap the **video window** to show and hide controls
- Move the window by **dragging to any part of the screen**
- **Drag the window off the right or left edge of the screen** to keep it out of sight
- Tap **X** to delete the window
- Tap  in tiny video window to restore the full FaceTime or video screen

Using Drag and Drop to Move Items
- Tap and hold the item or copy the text to select it
- Drag or move it to a new position within the app

Moving or Copying an item between Apps in Split Screen or Slide Over
- From two open apps on Split View or Slide Over, tap and hold the item or copy a text to select it

- **Next, move or drag** to destination app. A green circle with a white cross in it would appear to highlight where the item can be dropped

Copying an item to an app on the Home Screen or in the Dock

- **Tap and hold the item or highlight the text** to select it
- Use a second finger to **swipe up** from bottom edge of the screen to call up the **Dock** as you hold the item to be moved
- Move or drag the item over the destination app to launch it
- In case you decide not to move an item (s) anymore, just take away your finger before dragging or in the alternative, you can drag the item (s) off the screen

Dragging and Dropping Multiple items

- As you tap and hold the initial item, **use another finger** to tap additional items
- Next, **drag or move all** to the new location

Chapter 9: keyboard, Text and Typing

There are 4 ways or methods you could use to make inputs to your iPad. You can use the onscreen keyboard, an external keyboard, an Apple Pencil or dictation

Using the Onscreen Keyboard
- Launch the **onscreen keyboard** by tapping the text field. Tap the keys to type words
- You can use **QuickPath** to make inputs by sliding from one letter to another without lifting the finger. Lift your finger to end a word
- If you prefer to use one hand to type, you can drag the smaller keyboard from screen bottom. Pinch open to return to the full or default size keyboard

Using the Onscreen Keyboard as a Trackpad
- With one finger, tap and hold the **space bar** so that the keyboard turns light gray in color
- **Drag or move the keyboard** around to move the insertion point
- If you want to select text with handles, **keep touching and holding the keyboard** till handles show on the insertion point and move your fingers
- If you want to use the **trackpad** to move the insertion point, drag or move it to a new location before the handles show

Drag around the keyboard to move the insertion point.

using Accented Letters While Typing
- As you type, just tap and hold the letter, number or symbol related to the character you want

Using Predictive Text and Auto Correction

- As you type, tap and hold the smiling face in between the numbers button and the microphone symbol at bottom left on the onscreen keyboard.
- Tap **Keyboard Settings**
- Next turn typing features on or off

Using the dictating Function of iPad

- First switch on dictation by going to **Settings**
- tap **General,**
- tap **Keyboard**
- turn on **Enable Dictation**
- To dictate text, tap the **microphone icon** on the **onscreen keyboard** and then start speaking
- To add punctuation, say it as a word
- Tap ⌨ when you finish

Selecting and Editing Text

Depending on what you want to do, there are 3 ways to select text:

- To highlight a word, **Double-tap it with a finger**
- To highlight a paragraph, **Triple-tap with one finger**
- To highlight a line, sentence or text block, **touch and hold the first word in the block and drag to the last word.**
- You can **Cut, Paste, Copy, Replace** etc

Inserting Text Via Typing

- Tap on the section or point where you want to insert text. The cursor should appear there
- You can drag the insertion point to move it
- Next, type the text

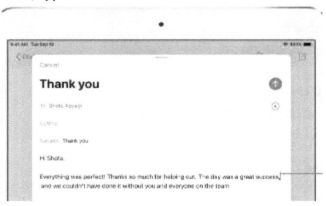

Adding or Removing a Keyboard

- Launch **Settings.** Tap **General.** Tap **Keyboard**
- Tap **Keyboards** and you can now add or remove a keyboard
- To add a keyboard, tap **Add New Keyboard** and select one from the list
- To remove, tap **Edit** and tap ⊖ next to the keyboard to remove. Tap **Delete.** Tap **Done**

Changing to Another Keyboard

- From the onscreen keyboard, **touch and hold** ☺ or ⊕ and tap the **keyboard name**
- If you are using an external keyboard, press and hold **Control** and tap the **space bar** to move between English and other keyboards

Chapter 10: AirDropping Items

The AirDrop is a function or feature of the iPad pro that allows you to securely send stuff like videos, music, websites, photos, etc to nearby Apple devices. AirDrop uses both Wi-Fi and Bluetooth and both have to be turned on.

Using AirDrop to send an item

Make sure you are signed in to your Apple ID

- Open the item
- Tap ⬆️
- Tap **Share**
- Tap **AirDrop**
- Tap the ellipsis ••• or if there's any other button that shows the sharing options for the app, tap it
- Next, tap from the sharing options row
- Tap the **profile picture** of an AirDrop user close to you. In the eventuality that the recipient is not recognized as a nearby AirDrop user, the person can go to **Control Center** and let AirDrop to receive items
- To send to a Mac user, the user must allow set their system to be discoverable in AirDrop in the finder

Receiving items via AirDrop

- Launch **Control Center** and tap . Alternatively, you can touch and hold the group of controls at top left
- On the next screen, tap **Contacts Only** or **Everyone** to select those that you want to receive items from

Chapter 11: Mark up

While using supported apps, including mail, Notes, Books, etc, you can annotate photos, sketch ideas, screen shots, PDF, write notes etc by using drawing tools.

Drawing or Writing in markup supported Apps
- From the Markup tool bar, tap the pencil, marker or pen
- Next, use your Apple Pencil to write or draw
- If the Markup bar is not evident in a supported app, you can tap

  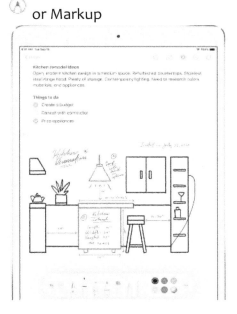 or Markup

Drawing a Shape

The markup tool allows you to draw geometrically perfect shapes for diagrams and sketches including lines, circles, etc

- From the **Markup bar,** tap the **pencil, pen or marker tool**
- Next, proceed to **draw a shape** in one fluid movement and then pause. A perfect rendition of the shape will become evident.
- If you much rather keep the one you drew, tap

Showing, Hiding and Moving the Toolbar
- While in a supported app, tap the **pencil tip within a circle symbol** or **Markup** and the following options can be done:

- Drag the **toolbar** to any part of the screen edge to move the Markup tool bar
- Tap the **ellipsis in a circle** and switch on **Auto-minimize** to shrink the toolbar when entering text or drawing
- Tap the **gray pencil tip in a circle** symbol to completely hide the toolbar

Adding Typed Text and Shapes

To include typed text in Notes, you can do so without using the Markup toolbar by following the step below:

- Close the **Markup toolbar** if its open by tapping the gray pencil tip in a circle symbol
- Next, tap in the note and type using either the onscreen or wireless keyboard. You can also use **Apple Pencil** and **Scribble** to enter text

To add and Edit typed Text in Supported Apps:
- While in the **Markup toolbar, tap the cross in a circle symbol** and tap **Next**
- Next, **Double-tap** the **text box**
- Enter text via the keyboard

Erasing an Error

- To do this, **Double-tap** the **eraser** in the **Markup toolbar**
- Based on what you want to do, you have the following options:
  1. Select **pixel Eraser** to erase pixels. Do this by scrubbing over the error using a finger or Apple Pencil
  2. Select **Object Eraser** to erase an object and touch the object with your finger or Apple Pencil

Adding and Adjusting shapes in Supported Apps

- From the **Markup toolbar,** tap the cross in a circle and select a shape

- Based on your intentions, use any of the following steps to adjust the shape:
  1. If you want to move any shape, Drag it
  2. If you want to resize any shape, Drag any blue dot along the outline
  3. If you want to change the outline color, tap a color in the color picker
  4. If you want to fill the shape with color, tap and select an option and color
  5. If you want to adjust the form of an arrow or speech bubble shape, Drag the green dot
  6. If you want to Delete or duplicate a shape, tap on it and choose an option

Adding your Signature

- Tap the **cross within a circle** in the **Markup toolbar** and select **Signature**
- Based on your intentions you have the following options:
  1. If you want to add a new signature, tap **Add or remove Signature,** tap the **cross or plus sign** and use Apple Pencil or any finger to sign
  2. If you want to use an already existing signature, tap the preferred one. Navigate down to view all signatures
  3. If you like the signature, tap **Done.** If you don't, tap **Clear** to sign a new one

Chapter 12: Control Center

From the control center, you can access to useful controls or apps such as volume, screen brightness, Do Not Disturb etc

Opening and Closing Control Center
- To launch the Control Center, you can swipe down from top right edge
- To close it, swipe upwards from the bottom of your screen

Accessing More Controls from Control Center
- To view and have access to additional options, touch and hold a control

Adding and Organizing Controls
- Launch **Settings**
- Tap **Control Center**
- If you want to add a control, tap the **white cross in a green circle**
- If you want to remove a control, **tap the white dash in a red circle**
- If you want to reorganize controls, touch the **3 long dashes** next to a control and drag it to a new location

Deactivating Access to Control Center in Apps

- Launch **Settings**
- Tap **Control center**
- Switch off **Access Within Apps**

Chapter 13: Notifications and Do not Disturb

The notifications function on your device keeps you up to date and advises you on stuff that's come in like email, messages, missed call event dates etc. You can see and respond to notifications from either the lock screen or from the notifications center.

Accessing your Notifications

- From the middle of the lock screen, **swipe upwards**
- You can also **swipe downwards** when you have other screens open. **Navigate upwards** to view and respond to previous notifications
- **Swipe upwards** from the screen bottom or press the Home button to close the notifications center when you are done

Responding to Notifications

To respond to notifications, you have the following options:

- **Tap** on a **specific notification** to open and reply
- If the iPad pro is locked, **touch and hold** a notification to view and respond to it
- If an app gives access to quick actions, **touch and hold** a notification to view it and do a **quick action response**. You can equally swipe left on the notification and tap **View**
- If you have notifications grouped together, **tap the group** to view them singly. **Tap on Show Less** to close the group again

Other Options

- If you want to clear every notification, **swipe Left and tap Clear** or **Clear All**. To clear all notifications in the Notification Center, **tap X** and tap **Clear**
- If a notification drops when you are using another app, **pull downwards** to view and respond. To dismiss it, **swipe upwards**
- **Swipe left** on a notification or notifications group **and tap Manage and tap Turn off** to deactivate notifications for an app or notifications group
- If you prefer to have all your notifications routed to the notifications center, **swipe left** from any notification, tap **Manage,** tap **Deliver Quietly**

Changing Notifications Settings
- Launch **Settings**
- Tap **Notifications**
- Tap **Show Previews** and choose an option from **Always, When Unlocked, or Never**
- Next, tap **Back** and **tap an app** below Notification style
- Turn **Allow Notifications** on or off.
- Select where and how the notifications are to appear, e.g, lock screen or notifications center
- If you want, you can choose how you want the notifications grouped by tapping **Notification Grouping** and select from grouping **By App** or **Automatic.** You can also turn off grouping by selecting **off**

Showing Recent Notifications on the Lock Screen
- Launch **Settings. Tap Touch ID & Passcode**
- Enter the **Passcode**
- Turn on **Notification Center** from below Allow Access When Locked

Silencing All Notifications/Activating Do Not Disturb
- Launch **Settings**
- Tap **Do Not Disturb.**
- Turn on **Do Not Disturb**
- Alternatively, launch **Control Center** and tap the 🌙 to turn on **Do Not Disturb**

Allowing Calls with Do Not Disturb Activated
- Launch **Settings.** Tap **Do Not Disturb**
- You have the following options:
  1. To allow calls from FaceTime and Wi-Fi calls from selected groups, Tap **Allow Calls From**
  2. To allow repeated calls from a caller, Turn on **Repeated Calls**

Allowing Emergency Contacts Calls with Do Not Disturb
- Launch **Contacts.** Select a **Contact** and tap **Edit**

- Next, tap **Ringtone** or **Text Tone** and switch on **Emergency Bypass**

Chapter 14: widgets

Add widgets to your home screen to view information from your most used apps from a glance. For e.g headlines, weather, events, etc.

Today view

- To access or launch the **Today View, swipe right** from the left edge of the Home or Lock screen

Today View widgets on your Home screen

- Keep your iPad pro in landscape position.
- Launch **Today View.**
- Touch and hold the **Home Screen background** until the apps start to shake
- Next, switch on **Keep on Home Screen** and tap **Done**

Adding widgets from the widget gallery

- Launch **Today view.**
- **Touch and hold Home screen** till apps start to shake
- Next, tap ╋ at screen top to launch the **widget gallery**
- Navigate to find a widget. **Tap on it** and **swipe** to select a size
- Tap **Add Widget** and tap **Done**

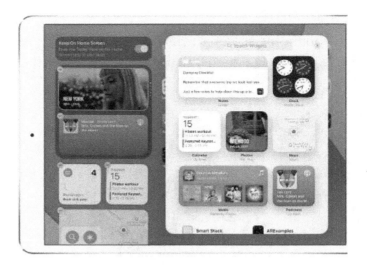

Repositioning or removing widgets
- Keep iPad pro in landscape position.
- Launch **Today View**
- **Touch and hold** Home screen background till apps begin to shake
- Chose from any of the two options below:
    1. Tap on a widget and tap **Remove**
    2. Move or drag a widget to a new position in Today View

Customizing a Widget
- **Touch and hold** a widget to launch a **quick actions** menu from your home screen
- Next, tap **Edit Widget** or **Edit Stack** and select options
- **Tap Home screen** background when you finish

Removing Today View from your Home screen
- Hold the Home screen background till apps start shaking
- Next turn off Keep on Home Screen and tap Done

Allowing Access to Today View if iPad pro is Locked
- Launch **Settings**
- Tap **Touch ID & Passcode**
- Key in **Passcode**
- Switch on **Today View** from below **Allow Access When Locked**

Chapter 15: iOS 14 features

The iOS 14 operating system is the latest for the Apple line up and features some new functions and capabilities designed to enable users have access better productivity.

Getting App Clips

You can use an app clip to get access to apps that you need. it's a small discoverable part of an app. You can use app clips for doing tasks like ordering food, renting a bike etc

- When you see an app clip link, **tap on it**
- Next, use your iPad pro camera to scan the **QR code** shown at the physical location
- To remove app clips, follow the steps below:
    1. launch **Settings**,
    2. tap **App Clips**.
    3. Tap **Remove All App Clips**

Using your iPad proto Make and Receive Calls

you can route calls to your iPad pro through your iPhone. To do this you must set up FaceTime and Apple ID on both devices. Make sure you set up the iPhone first before your iPad. Your iPad pro must be near the phone and connected to Wi-Fi. Follow the steps below:

- Launch **Settings** on your iPhone.
- Tap **Cellular.**
- Select a **SIM** or **line**
- Next tap **Calls on other Devices.**
- Switch on **Allow Calls on Other Devices**.
- Select your iPad. You can also tap **Wi-Fi Calling**.
- Switch on **Add Wi-Fi Calling for Other Devices**
- Next, from your iPad, **set up FaceTime** and sign in to **the same Apple ID** as with your iPhone
    1. Launch **Settings**
    2. Tap **FaceTime**
    3. Switch on **FaceTime** and **Calls from iPhone.** You may have to turn on Wi-Fi calling if require

- To make a call, tap a **phone number** from your **contacts, FaceTime,** etc. you can also do that from **FaceTime** by entering a contact or phone number and tap the call icon or symbol
- To receive a call, **tap or swipe the notification** to answer or ignore

Using scribble on iPad

The scribble function is handy for entering text, responding to a message, taking a reminder, etc without using the onscreen keyboard. You use the Apple Pencil to do this.

Entering Text with Apple Pencil from any Text Field
- Just use the pencil to write in any text field. Your handwriting would be automatically converted to typed text
- Tap the **scribble toolbar** to use an action shortcut

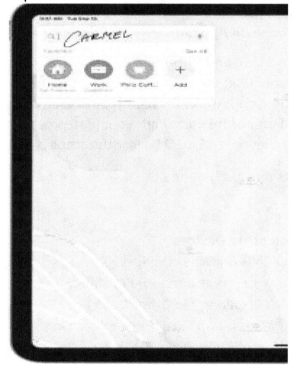

Entering Text with Apple Pencil in Notes
- Open the **Notes app.**
- Tap the **pencil tip in a circle symbol** to view the **Markup toolbar**

- Tap the **Handwriting tool** that represented by a **pencil tip without a circle** to the left of the pen
- Next use the **Apple Pencil** to write. Your handwriting would be changed to typed text

Using Apple Pencil to Highlight and make Changes to Text
- If you want to delete a word, **scratch it out**
- If you want to select text, draw a circle around it or underline it to view editing options
- You can **double-tap a word** to select it
- If you want to join or separate characters, **draw a vertical line between them**
- If you want to insert text, **touch and hold the area** and a space would open. Write in it
- **Triple-tap a word** in a paragraph to select the paragraph or alternatively drag your pencil over the paragraph

Using the Notes Function to Draw or Write
- Open the **Notes app**. Use your **Apple Pencil** to write or draw. To use your finger, **tap the pencil tip in a circle**
- Use the **Markup tools** to make adjustments such as color or tools
- **Drag or move the resize handle** to the left up or down to adjust the handwriting area

Selecting and Editing Drawings and Handwriting

- **Tap the pencil tip** in the **Markup toolbar** between the eraser and ruler
- Use the methods described below to select drawings and writings based on your preference and intentions:
    1. To expand a selection, **touch and hold and then drag**
    2. To select a word, **double-tap it**
    3. To highlight a sentence, **triple-tap it**
- Based on your intention, tap the selection and select **Cut, Copy, Delete, Duplicate, Copy as Text or Insert Space Above**
- To use handwritten addresses, phone numbers, dates etc, **tap the underlined text**

Guides Feature of Maps App

Users now have the added possibility of discovering wonderful places to eat, shop and explore around the world. This new feature is enabled by trusted brands and partners and is continually updated to reflect new places. To use this feature, follow the steps below:

- Tap on the **Search field** to open or launch a guide and one of the options listed below can be selected:
    1. Tap on a cover from beneath Editor's picks
    2. Tap **See All** and select an option from top of the **All Guides** card and tap on a cover
    3. You can swipe down, select a publisher and tap a cover

    Use one of these options:

- You can **save** by tapping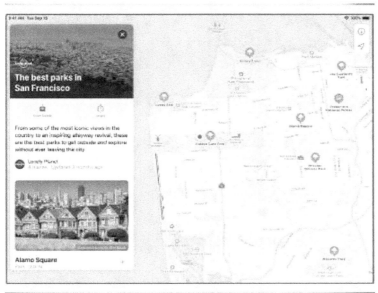
- You can decide to **share** by tapping
- You can decide to add one of its destinations to **My Guides.** To do so, tap and choose of your guides
- If you want to return to the search field, tap

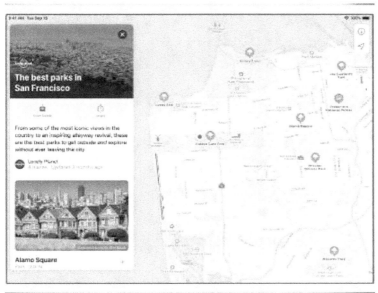

Cycling Directions from current Maps Location
Use one of the following options:

- To use Siri, say something like**, "Hey Siri, give me cycling directions to the church"**
- You can tap your **destination,** tap **Directions** and finally, tap the **bicycle** icon
- You can also **touch and hold** any spot on the map, **tap Directions** and tap the **bicycle icon**
- You can tap **Go** for your preferred route

Chapter 16: using iPad pro to control home accessories

Apple has built in the added capability to allow you the luxury of controlling your home appliances and electrical fittings or accessories from within the **Home app** and **Control Center** on your iPad. You can also set up and monitor activity zones, use compatible video cameras and door bells to know when tagged visitors show up on your doorstep. The kind of controls you get is based on the type of accessory

Adding an Accessory to Home on your iPad

- First, make sure that the accessory is on, connected to a power source and is on your Wi-Fi
- Launch the **Home app**
- Tap **Home** in the **sidebar** and tap ⊕
- Next, tap **Add Accessory** and follow the instructions on your display to finish

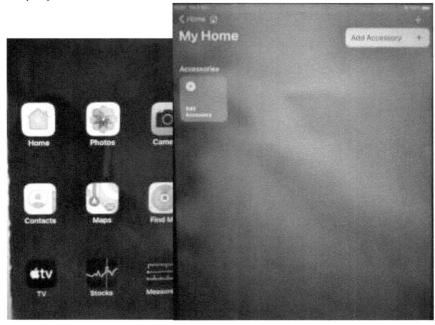

Changing an Accessory's Location Assignment

- Go to the **sidebar** in the **Home app**
- Highlight or select its room of current assignment
- **Touch and hold** its button and swipe up

- Next, tap **Room** and select a room
- Switch on **Include in Favorites** to add it to the **Home tab**
- If you want to reposition your favorites, tap the **house icon** and tap **Edit screen**. Move or drag the accessory buttons into the new placements and tap **Done** when you are done

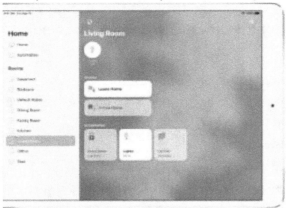

Using the Home app to control accessories

- From the **sidebar,** tap **Home** or a **room**
- Next, tap the **button** for controlling the accessory to turn on or off
- You have option of **touching and holding** the button till the controls come into view

Using Control Center to control Accessories

- Launch **Settings**
- Tap **Control Center** under **General** in the **Settings** list
- Turn on **Show Home Controls**
- Tap a **button** to turn an accessory on or off or **touch and hold** the button till controls show

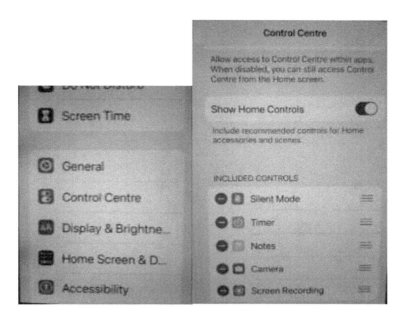

Editing Home Accessories

- **Touch and hold** the **accessory button**
- Swipe up and execute one of the two options below:
    1. If you want to change the name of an accessory, tap ✕ to wipe the old name and enter the new one
    2. If you want to substitute an accessory's icon for another, tap on the icon next to the accessory name and choose a new icon

Grouping and controlling Accessories

- To group accessories together, **touch and hold** an accessory, **swipe up** on the screen and tap **Group with Other Accessories**
- Next, tap the **accessory** you want to group with the **accessory**
- Enter a **name** for the group in the **name field**
- **Tap done**

Viewing your Home status

Use this function to see and correct issues in your home. For e.g, an unlocked front or garage door, a light still on at the wrong time etc

- Launch the **Home app**
- Tap **Home** in the **sidebar**

- Tap on any of the **round buttons** that show just below your home name
- View and correct any issue

Setting up and using Face Recognition

You need a compatible camera and/or doorbell for this feature

- To set up, add the accessory to the **Home app** especially if you are setting the camera or door bell up for the first time
- While in the **Recognize Familiar Faces** card, switch on **Face Recognition**
- Tap **Continue**
- Select who can access your photo. Choose from **Never, Only Me or Everyone in this Home**
- Tap **continue** and finish the camera or doorbell setup
- In case you already have a camera or doorbell you prefer to use, follow the steps below:
    1. Tap on it in the **Home tab**. Next, tap
    2. Tap **Face Recognition**
    3. Activate or switch on **Face Recognition**
    4. From your photo library, select who can access it

Using Face Recognition to identify Visitors and Add them to your Photo Library

To add visitors that are not included in your photo library, follow steps below:

- Activate **Face Recognition**
- Launch the **Home app** and tap **Home** in the **sidebar**
- Next, tap the **camera or doorbell**
- Tap **Face Recognition**
- Tap an unidentified person listed under **Recent** and tap **Add Name**
- Add their **name**
- Select if you want to be informed if they are detected by your camera or doorbell

Receiving Notifications from Camera or Doorbells

- Go to the **Home** app
- Tap the **house icon** and tap **Home Settings**
- Next, tap **Cameras and Doorbells**
- Specify the Camera you have in mind by **tapping on it**
- Switch on **Notifications on this iPad**
- Select to get notifications when a clip is recorded

Enabling others to view Faces in your Library

- Activate Face Recognition
- Launch the **Home app**
- Tap the **house icon** and tap **Home Settings**
- Tap **Cameras and Doorbells** and tap **Face Recognition**
- Finally, tap your **photo library** and tap **Everyone in this Home**

Organizing Rooms or Parts of your House into Zones

This would make it easier to control different parts of your house via Siri. After grouping areas of your home, to control the areas is as easy as asking Siri to perform functions such as turning the lights on or off in one or more of those areas.

- Open the **Home app** and tap **Home Settings**
- Tap **Zone** and tap an existent zone

- You can tap **Create New** to include the room to a new zone

Editing a Room

Change a room's name, add it to a zone etc. do it with the steps below:

- Tap the **House icon.**
- Tap **Room Settings**
- Finally, tap a room and make changes

Sending a Message

- Tap the **blue pencil and pad icon or symbol** at top left of screen to begin a new message.
- Next, key in the recipient **contact name, Apple ID or phone number**.
- Call up the text up field, type the message and tap the **white arrow in a blue circle** at right of the text field to send the message

Reply to a Message

- Tap the **particular conversation** from the messages list
- Next, tap the **text field** and tap the reply or response
- Alternatively, use the **search field** to locate particular contacts, message content etc
- When you are done, tap the **white arrow in the blue circle** at right of the text field to send

Replying to a Specific Message in a Conversation

- To do this, you have either of two options:

1. You can **touch and hold** a message
2. You can **double-tap** a message
- Next, **tap out your response** and hit the **blue send icon with white arrow** at right of text field

Pinning and Unpinning a Conversation
- To pin any conversation, **swipe right on it** and tap the tack or pin icon or symbol
- Next, to prioritize a conversation for prompt response, **touch and hold it** and move to top of list
- To unpin a conversation, repeat the first two steps in reverse order

Switching from a Messages Conversation to a FaceTime or Audio Call
- While in a **conversation**, tap the **profile picture** or the name at top of the conversation
- Next tap **FaceTime or audio**

Copying a contact in conversations
- Open a **specific conversation.** Start typing the **contact's name** in the text field
- Tap on the **contact's name** when it shows and send. In the alternative, type **@** and type the **name of the recipient** or contact

Changing a group name and photo
- Tap the **name** or **number** at top of the conversation
- Tap the ⓘ at top right.
- Next, select **Change Name and Photo**

Using Business Chat
Use this message feature to communicate with businesses to get make enquiries and get help.

- First, use apps like **Maps, Search, Safari or Siri** to locate or find **a specific business** you want to chat with

- Next initiate a conversation by **tapping on a chat link** in the search results

Sending Memoji and Memoji Stickers

- While in a conversation, tap 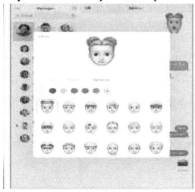. Next, tap a **Memoji** in the top row to display the stickers
- **Tap the sticker** to include it in the message. You have the option of including a comment if you want. When you finish, tap the **blue send button or icon**
- As another option, you can **touch and hold a sticker** and move or drag it on top of a message

Creating your very own Memoji

- While you are in a conversation, tap and **tap the blue cross in a light blue circle**
- Next, tap each feature and select from the options and create you custom Memoji
- When you finish, tap **Done**
- If you want to **edit, delete or duplicate a Memoji**, tap , next, **tap the Memoji** and tap the **ellipsis in a light blue circle**

Taking a Photo

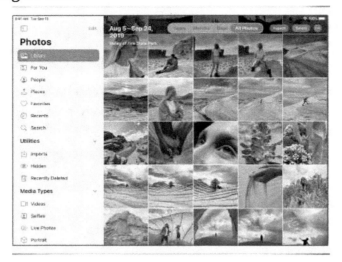

- On the Home screen, **tap the camera icon** to launch the camera. Alternatively, **swipe left on the Lock Screen** to launch the camera
- To take a photo, with the camera activated, tap the white **shutter button**. you can equally use any of the **volume buttons** to take the photo
- To view, select or use the flash setting, tap the **flash symbol** that looks like lightning and then select from **Auto, On** or **Off**
- If you want to use the timer to take a photo, tap the **timer icon** and select between 3 or 10 seconds. When the countdown elapses, the photo will be taken.
- Pinch the screen to **zoom in or out** or use the **slider** on the left to do so

Taking a panoramic shot

- Launch **Camera.** Select **Pano Mode.** Tap the **white shutter button**
- Next, pan slowly, following the arrow's direction. Make sure you keep the arrow on the center line
- When you are done, tap the **Shutter button**

Taking a selfie

- Launch the **Camera**. Switch to the front camera by tapping the **camera icon**
- Stabilize the camera in front of you and tap the **Shutter button** or press any of the **volume buttons** to take the photo
- To use the portrait setting to take a selfie, activate the **portrait setting.** Doing this would automatically activate the front camera. Use the **yellow portrait box** to frame yourself. Tap the **shutter button** when you are ready

Taking and viewing burst shots

- Launch **Camera**. Select photo or square mode
- Next, touch and hold the **Shutter button** to shoot the burst shots
- When you are done, lift your finger from the shutter button
- Choose photos to keep by opening the burst shot, tapping the **Burst thumbnail** and tapping **Select**
- For each photo you want to retain, tap the circle at lower right corner and tap **Done** when you finish
- If you want to delete the burst shot photos, tap on the thumbnail and tap the **blue delete or dustbin icon**

Taking and viewing live photos

Use the live photo feature to capture events preceding the shot and the post shot event

- Launch **Camera.** Select Photo mode
- Next, tap ⊚ to activate Live Photos on or off. When it's on, its yellow
- Use the **shutter button** when ready to take the picture
- To do this, open it, **touch and hold** the photo to play it

Recording a Video

- Launch **Camera.** Select **Video mode.** Tap the **red Record button** to begin.
- To stop recording, tap the **record button** again or any of the **volume buttons**
- To play a video**, tap on it** to begin to play it in full screen mode. Use the **player controls** beneath the video to do any of the following: **play, pause, mute, unmute.**

Recording a Slow-motion Video

- Launch **Camera.** Select **Slo-mo mode**
- Next, tap the **red Record button** to begin or any of the **volume buttons.**
- To stop the recording, **tap the record button** again or any **volume button**
- If you want to alter the **Slo-mo** recording settings, launch **Settings,** tap **Camera, tap Record Slo-mo** and make the desired changes

Capturing a Time-Lapse Video

- Launch **Camera.** Select **Time-lapse Mode**
- Next, set up the iPad pro where you want to capture anything for a specified amount of time
- The third step is to tap the **Record button** to begin the recording
- To stop the recording, tap the **record button** again

Filtering photos in Albums

- To filter photos, tap the **ellipsis in the circle** and tap **Filter**
- Next, select your preference in filtering the photos and videos in any album and tap **Done**
- If you want to remove a filter from an album, tap the **blue circle with 3 dashes** inside it. **Tap All Items** and tap **Done**

Using Folders to Organize Albums

- From the left edge of the screen, **swipe or tap** ▭ to reveal the sidebar
- Next, tap **All Albums** below My Albums
- Tap the **blue add cross symbol** and tap **New Folder**
- Launch the Folder, tap **Edit** and tap the **blue cross icon** to create new albums or folders within the folder

Viewing Photos

- To view or see individual photos, tap the photo thumbnail to display it in full screen.
- While its displayed, you have the following options depending on your intention:
  1. **Double tap or pinch out** or in to zoom in or out to examine the photo in great detail
  2. If you want to share the photo, tap ⬆ and select from the options how you want to share
  3. If you want to add the photo to your favorite collection, tap the love icon or symbol
  4. To return back, tap the **blue symbol** at top extreme left of screen or drag down the photo

Tap a thumbnail to view a photo.

Customizing and playing a Slideshow

- Open **Photos.**
- Tap **Select.**
- Next, start selecting each photo to be included in the slide show and then tap
- Select or tap **Slideshow** from the list of options
- Next, tap on the screen and tap **Options** to alter the theme, music etc

Chapter 19: FaceTime

Face time is a video calling app that allows users or participants to combine audio and video for better communications.

Making a FaceTime Call

- Open **FaceTime** app.
- Tap the **blue cross shaped** Add symbol that's situated at **screen top**
- Next, enter the name or number of the person you want to speak to in the **entry field** at top. In the alternative, you can open contacts by tapping the **blue cross within a blue circle** to select the person from there
- To make the call, tap the **video call icon** that looks like a video or camcorder.
- If you prefer to make an Audio FaceTime call, tap the **call icon** or symbol

Making a Group FaceTime Call

- Follow step one as outlined in making a FaceTime call above
- Type the names or numbers of those to be participants in the call in the **entry field** at top
- Follow steps 3 and 4 as above as applicable

Swipe up to add another person to the call.

Tap to hang up.

Tap to add stickers or other fun effects.

Starting a Group FaceTime call from a Group Messages Conversation

- While in a group messages conversation, tap or select the **names or profile pictures** at the top of the conversation
- To start the call, tap **FaceTime**

Adding a New Participant to a Call

- While in a FaceTime call, **tap on the screen** to launch the controls.
- Swipe upwards from the top of the controls and tap **Add Person**
- Next, type the **name, Apple ID, or phone number** of the new participant in the entry field
- Finally, tap **Add Person to FaceTime**

Exiting a Group FaceTime Call

- If any participant desires to exit the group FaceTime call, the participant just taps the **white Asterix in a red circle**

Chapter 20: family sharing

Use family sharing to share subscriptions, games, purchases etc. A family group can have up to five members apart from the family member that sets up the family group. The founding family member decides the stuff to be shared.

Setting up Family Sharing

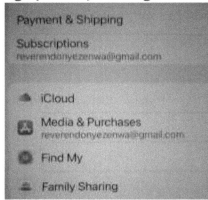

- The founding member signs in with Apple ID
- Next, **Launch Settings**
- Tap **your name.**
- Tap **Family Sharing**
- Follow instructions to set up family group
- Next, **tap a feature** to be shared in your family group and obey the instructions to finish

Adding a New Family Member

Only the founding member can add new members. To do this, follow steps outlined below:

- Launch **Settings**
- Tap **your name**
- Tap **Family Sharing**
- Tap **Add Member**

- Next Tap **Invite People** and obey the instructions to complete adding the new member

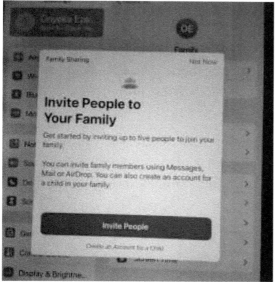

Setting up an Apple ID for a child

- Launch **Settings**
- Tap **your name.**
- tap **Family Sharing**
- Tap **Add Member.**
- Tap **Create an Account for a Child** and follow the onscreen prompts to complete the set up

Viewing what you are sharing in your Family Group

- Launch **Settings.** Tap **your name.** Tap **Family Sharing**
- Tap **a feature.** You can now review and make changes to the sharing settings

Exiting or Deactivating Family Sharing

- Launch **Settings.** Tap **your name.** Tap **Family Sharing**
- To end the group, tap **Stop Family Sharing**
- To exit the family sharing group, tap **Stop Using Family Sharing**

Downloading Shared Purchases from iTunes Store

- Launch **iTunes store.** Tap **Purchased**

- Next tap **My Purchases** at top left
- Select the **family member**

- Tap a **category** at screen top, tap a purchased item and tap to get it

Downloading shared purchases from App Store
- Launch **App store**
- Tap the **picture frame or your profile picture** at the top right
- Next, tap **Purchased**. Choose a family member. Select a purchased item and tap the blue cloud with a downward pointing arrow to download it

Downloading shared purchases from Apple Books
- Launch the **Books** app

- Tap the **profile picture** icon at top right

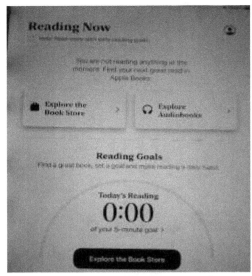

- Tap a **family member's name** from **Family Purchases.**
- Tap a **category**
- Next, tap **All, Recent Purchases** or a genre and tap the cloud with an arrow icon to download

Downloading Shared Purchases from the Apple TV app
- Launch the **Apple TV app**
- Next, Library, tap **Family Sharing**, select a Family member
- Tap a **category or genre**
- Tap a **purchased item** and tap the download icon to get it

Deactivating purchase Sharing
- Launch **Settings.** Tap **your name.** Tap **Family Sharing**
- Tap **purchase Sharing.** Switch off **Share Purchase Sharing**

Activating Ask to Buy For Children
- Launch **Settings.** Tap **your name.** tap **Family Sharing**
- Next, tap the **name of the child**
- switch on **Ask to Buy**
- If you are activating it for the first time, Tap **Add Child** or **Create A Child Account** and follow the directions

Activating Apple Cash Family for a Child
- Launch **Settings**

- Tap Y**our name.**
- Tap **Family Sharing**
- Next, tap **Apple Cash.**
- Tap the **Child's name.**
- Tap **Set Up Apple Cash** and obey the directions to finish the set up
- If you are setting it up for the first time, follow step 3 as above in Activating Ask to Buy

Sharing Subscriptions and iCloud storage with family members
- Launch **Settings**
- Tap **your name.**
- Tap **Family Sharing**
- Tap a **subscription** and follow the onscreen directions to complete the setup

Setting Up your iPad pro to be Found
- Launch **Settings.**
- Tap **Privacy.**
- Activate **Location Services**
- Next, launch **Settings.**
- Tap **your name.** Tap **Find My**

- Tap **Find My iPad.**
- Switch on **Find My iPad.**
- **Tap** Find My Network.
- Tap **Send Last Location**

Sharing your Location with your Family Members
- Launch **Settings.** Tap **your name.** Tap **Family Sharing**
- Tap **Location Sharing.** Turn on **Share My Location**

Chapter 21: using your iPad pro with other Apple Products

You can use your iPad pro in various ways to interface with any other Apple product you have own such as iPhone, Mac, iPod touch etc. you can also connect your iPad proto Windows PC using a USB cable to execute functions. Find some of the ways you can use your iPad pro with other devices below:

Using your iPad proas a Hotspot

- Launch **Settings**
- Tap **Cellular**
- Tap **Personal Hotspot**
- Switch on **Allow Others to join**

If you want to change the password for your iPad pro Hotspot, do the following:

- Launch **Settings**
- Tap **Cellular**
- Tap **Personal Hotspot**
- Next, tap **Wi-Fi Password** and effect password change
- Tap **Done**

If you want to personalize your Hotspot name, do the following:

- From **Settings**
- Tap **General**
- Tap **About**
- Tap **Name**
- Change the name to the one you prefer
- Tap **Done**

If you want to deactivate personal Hotspot and disconnect connected devices, do the following:

- Launch **Settings**
- Tap **Cellular**
- Tap Personal **Hotspot**
- Switch off **Allow Others to Join**

Connecting other Apple Devices to your iPad pro Hotspot

- From the other device, launch **Settings**
- Next, turn on the **Wi-Fi**
- Select your **iPad pro Hotspot** when it the other device detects it
- Enter the **Hotspot password** on the connecting device if required
- Tap **Ok**

Alternatively, to set up both devices so that instant Hotspot connects them without asking for a password, do the following:

- Sign in with the same **Apple ID** on both devices
- Turn on the **Bluetooth** function of both devices
- Next, turn on the **Wi-Fi** function of both devices
- A connection should be established between both devices

Tethering your Mac or PC to your iPad pro Hotspot

You have three options for connecting your Mac to your iPad pro Hotspot:

you can do it via **Wi-Fi, Bluetooth** or **USB.**

For a Wi-Fi connection, do the following:

- Make sure you are signed in with the same **Apple ID** on both your iPad pro and Mac
- next, activate your Wi-Fi on your Mac
- from your Mac, use the **Wi-Fi status menu** to select your iPad pro from the list of available networks

for a Bluetooth connection, follow the steps below:

- launch **Settings**, activate your iPad pro **Bluetooth** and use the **Bluetooth settings** to make sure that your iPad pro is discoverable
- Next, on your Mac or PC, also activate the **Bluetooth** function and follow the directions to establish a connection to your iPad pro hotspot

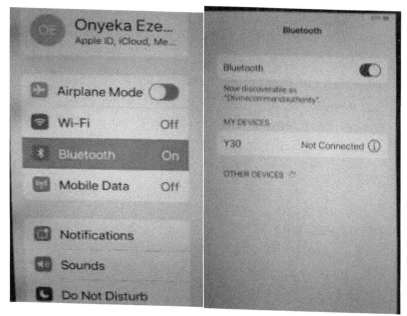

for a USB connection follow the steps outlined below:

- You need a Mac with a USB port and OS X 10.9 or later. For a PC, you need one with a USB port running windows 7 or later
- Next, establish a connection between your Mac or PC and the iPad pro using the right cable
- The type of cable you would use depends on the type of USB port your Mac or PC is equipped with. You may have to purchase the proper cable if it's not included with the accessories
- During the connection or set up phase, if you get an alert that says: **Trust this Computer?** you are to tap **Trust**
- Next, from your **PC or Mac's network preferences**, select **iPad pro** and configure the network settings

Using your iPad pro to Make and Receive Calls

Its possible for you to use your iPhone as a relay or medium to channel calls to your iPad. To do this, you have to sign in with the same Apple ID on the 2 devices. You must also set up FaceTime. Note that you will require iOS 9 or later for your iPhone and iPad pro OS 13 for your iPad

- Go to **Settings** on your iPhone

- Tap **Cellular**
- Select a line if your iPhone is equipped with a dual SIM capability
- Next, tap **Calls on Other Devices**
- Tap **Allow Calls on Other Devices** and select your iPad
- For you to make and receive calls with your iPad, the Wi-Fi must just be turned on and it must be near your iPhone

To Use Wi-Fi:

- Go to **Settings** on your iPhone
- Tap **Wi-Fi Calling**
- Turn on **Add Wi-Fi Calling for Other Devices**
- You will now be able to make and receive calls even if your phone is not close to you

Making or Receiving a Call on Your iPad

- If you want to make a call, tap a **phone number** from your **contacts, calendar, Message, Spotlight** or **Safari**
- To use FaceTime, open the **facetime app**, enter a **contact** or **phone number** and dial
- To receive calls, swipe or **tap the notification** to answer or decline the call

Using iPad pro as a Dual Display for your Mac

You can use your iPad proas a second display for your Mac. You can use a function called Sidecar to extend your workspace. With this you can use different apps on different screens or use the same app on both screens by a process termed mirroring. For you to use Sidecar, on your Mac, you need at least, macOS10.15 or later and iPadOS 13 or later

How to Use Sidecar

- Use the same **Apple ID** to sign in to your Mac and iPad
- Turn on the **Wi-Fi** and **Bluetooth** function of your Mac and iPad pro and make sure they are within Bluetooth range of each other or you can use USB cable to connect both devices
- Next, click on the **AirPlay menu** from your Mac and choose your iPad
- You now have any of the following functions:
    1. You can switch between using your iPad proas a mirrored or separate display. You can also decide to show or hide the side or touch bar on iPad
    2. Move windows to iPad pro by dragging a window to screen edge till the pointer shows on the iPad. In the alternative, you can hover the pointer over the green button at top left corner of the window and select Move to your iPad pro name
    3. Move windows back to Mac by repeating step two above in reverse order
    4. Use the **sidebar** on your iPad pro by tapping with your **finger** or **Apple Pencil** on the icons in sidebar to show or hide the menu bar, the Dock or the Key board
    5. Use the **Touch Bar** on iPad pro by tapping with finger or Apple Pencil on any button in the Touch Bar
    6. Use **Apple Pencil** on iPad proto select items such as menu commands, checkboxes or files
    7. You can still use your **fingers** to perform standard gestures on iPad pro such as **tap, Touch and hold, swipe, scroll and zoom**
    8. Switch between the Mac desktop and iPad pro Home Screen on your iPad. **Swipe up** from bottom to view the iPad pro **Home Screen** and tap the **Sidecar icon** in the **Dock** on your iPad proto view the Mac desktop
- To disconnect your iPad, tap the **Disconnect icon** at sidebar bottom

- To disconnect your iPad pro via the Mac, do it from the **Sidecar menu** in the **menu bar** and in **sidecar and display preferences** on your Mac

Changing Sidecar Preferences
- From your Mac, select **Apple menu**
- Next, tap **system Preferences**
- Click **Sidecar**

You can do any of the following:

1. You can decide to show, hide or move the sidebar on your iPad. To show the side bar, choose **Show Sidebar.** To hide it, deselect **Show Sidebar**. To move it, click on the **pop-up menu** and select a location
2. To do the same as above for the **Touch Bar** on your iPad, choose **Show Touch Bar** to view it. To hide it, deselect **Show Touch Bar**. To move it, click on the pop-up menu and select a new location
3. In the eventuality that you have more than one iPad, you have to specify or choose one to connect to your Mac. To do this, click on the **"Connect to" pop up menu** and then choose your preferred iPad

Handing off Tasks between Your iPad pro and Mac
You have the added flexibility of continuing your work on another device at the exact point that you left off on the device that you initially started with. This function or capability is possible with a lot of Apple apps and a number of third -party apps. Follow the directions as outlined below:

- Make sure that you are signed in to **Apple ID** on both devices
- Turn on the Bluetooth function of both devices from **Settings**
- Ensure that both devices are within Bluetooth range of each other
- To switch from Mac to your iPad, tap the **Handoff icon** at the right side of the Dock on your iPad

- To switch to your Mac from iPad, tap the **Handoff icon** that appears at the left end of the **Dock** or at the top and click the icon to resume working in the app

Deactivating Handoff on your Devices

- On your iPad, iPhone and iPod touch, launch **Settings.**
- Tap **General**

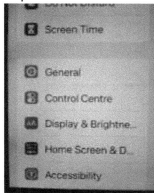

- Tap **AirPlay and Handoff**

- Switch button **to off**

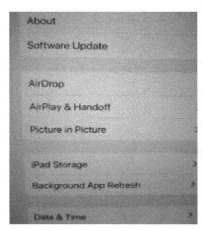
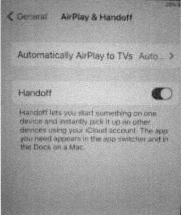

On your Mac:

- Select **Apple Menu**
- Click **System Preferences**
- Click **General**

- Turn off **Allow Handoff between this Mac and your iCloud devices**

Using the universal clipboard function to Cut, Copy and Paste between your Devices

The versatility afforded by the interfunctionality and interoperability that cuts across the Apple range of devices is such that you can cut or copy content from one device and paste it on another; say from your iPad proto your iPhone etc. Here's how:

- As usual, sign in to your devices with the same **Apple ID**
- Turn on **Wi-Fi** on the devices
- Turn on **Bluetooth** from **Settings** and make sure that they are within Bluetooth range
- Ensure that you have **Handoff** enabled on your devices
- To copy, **pinch closed with three fingers**
- To cut, **pinch closed with three fingers 2 times**
- To paste, **pinch open with 3 fingers**
- For a selection, **touch and hold** and then **tap Copy, Cut or Paste**

Syncing your Mac or PC with your iPad

Use syncing to keep your stuff updated across your Apple devices via iCloud. You can also use your windows PC to sign in to your iCloud account from iCloud.com and access your stuff. In case you don't feel like using iCloud, you can connect your iPad proto Mac or Windows PC and sync items such as music, photos and videos, contacts, calendars, movies, etc. Find how to do so below:

- Use **USB** to Connect your iPad proto Mac or PC
- From the **Finder sidebar** on your Mac, choose your iPad. You need macOS 15 or later. In the alternative, uses iTunes if your macOS is an early version
- Next, click the kind of content you want to sync from the window top
- Choose or select 'Sync [Content type] onto [device name]

- If you are interested in syncing more than one type of content, repeat steps 3 and 4 for each type of content and click **Apply**

Syncing Between your Windows PC and iPad

- Use a **USB cable** to link your iPad pro to your PC
- Launch **iTunes** on your PC
- Next, click on the **iPad pro button** near the top left of the iTunes window
- Choose or specify the kind of content you want to sync from the left sidebar
- Click on **Sync** to activate the sync function that kind of item
- If you are interested in syncing more than one type of content, repeat steps 3 and 4 and click **Apply**

Using Wi-Fi Syncing

- First, link your iPad pro to your Mac or PC via **USB cable**

For Mac, do the following:

- Select your iPad pro from the **Finder sidebar** on your Mac
- Click **General** at top of window
- Next, choose "**show this [device] when on Wi-Fi**"
- Click **Apply**
  Note that your Mac must be running macOS 15 or later or in the alternate, use iTunes to activate Wi-Fi syncing

For PC, follow the steps below:

- Launch **iTunes**
- Click the **iPad pro button** near the **top left** of the **iTunes window**
- Next, click **summary**
- Choose "**Sync with this [device] over Wi-Fi**
- Click **Apply**

Moving files between your iPad pro and Mac or PC

The iCloud drive helps you keep all your files up to date and you can access and transfer them across your devices using media such as mail and AirDrop. If you prefer to use other means, then you may consider moving the files via USB cable

Moving files between iPad pro and Mac

- Link your iPad pro and Mac **via USB or Wi-Fi** Connection
- Choose your iPad pro from the **Finder sidebar** on your **Mac**
- **From top of the Finder window,** click on **Files** and you can do one of the options outlined below:
    1. If you want to transfer files from Mac to iPad, **move or drag a file or file grouping** as the case may be**,** from a **finder window** onto an **app name** on the list
    2. If you want to move files from iPad proto Mac, click the **disclosure triangle** next to an **app name** to view its files on your iPad pro and then **drag or move** a specific file to a Finder window
- If you want to delete a file from your iPad, select it from under an **app name**, then press **Command-Delete** and click **Delete**

Moving Files Between your iPad pro and PC

- Link both devices with USB cable or Wi-Fi sync
- Launch **iTunes**
- Click the **iPad pro button** close to **top left** of **iTunes window**
- Next, click **File Sharing**
- Choose an app from the list and choose one of the 2 options below based on your intention:
    1. If you want to move a file from your iPad proto your PC, choose the file from the list to the right and click "**Save to**" Next, specify where the file should be saved and click **Save To**
    2. If you want to transfer a file from your PC to iPad, click **Add,** choose the file and click **Add**

Chapter 22: Troubleshooting
Shutting down and restarting iPad

Based on what type or model of iPad pro you have, use the right one from the following options to shut down and restart:

- press and maintain pressure on the top button till you see the **slider.** Drag or move the **slider** to shut down. To power it back on, press and hold **top button** till you view the Apple logo

- For other versions, press both the top button and any of the volume buttons at the same time till the **slider** comes into view. Move the **slider** to power off. To turn it back on, press and hold top button till the Apple logo displays

- To shut down your iPad pro from settings, launch **Settings.** Tap **General**. Tap **Shutdown.** Drag or move the slider. To turn back on, press and hold the top button till you view the Apple logo

Doing a Hard Restart

- press and maintain a hold on the **top button** and one of the volume buttons simultaneously. Release both buttons when the Apple logo appears
- For other versions, in one fluid motion, press and quickly let go of the **volume up** button, do the same for the **volume down** button, and press and hold the top button. when you see the Apple logo, let go of the button

Updating your iPad pro OS

You have 3 options. You can do it manually; you can set your iPad pro to update automatically whenever an update is available or you can use your computer

- to update automatically, launch **Settings**. Tap **General**. Tap **Software Update**
- next, tap **Customize Automatic Updates** and select to auto down load and install updates
- to update manually, launch **Settings,** tap **General**. Tap **Software Update**
- to use your computer**, connect** the **iPad pro** to the **computer. If** you have a Mac, from the **finder bar, choose your iPad.** Next, click **General** at the window top. Use iTunes to update iPad
- for windows PC, Launch **iTunes,** select your iPad pro at top left of the iTunes window. Click **Summary**. Next, click **Check for Update. Click Update** to install one if available

Backing up your iPad

Just like updating your iPad pro as above, you have 3 options for backing up your iPad. You can use iCloud, your Mac or windows PC

- **to use iCloud**, launch **Settings.**
- Tap **your name.** tap **iCloud Backup.**
- Activate **iCloud Backup.** To do it manually, tap **Back Up Now**

to use Mac, connect iPad proto your Mac with the USB cable.

- Select your **iPad pro** from the **Finder sidebar.**
- Click **General** from top of finder window.
- Next, opt for **Back up all of the data on your iPad pro to this Mac**. Decide to encrypt or not.
- Click **Back up Now**

to use windows PC, launch **iTunes.**

- Choose your **iPad pro** from **top left** of the **iTunes** window
- Next, click **Summary**
- Click **Back Up Now**
- Select **Encrypt local backup** if you want. Type a **password**. Click **Set Password**

Returning your iPad pro Settings to factory Settings
- launch **Settings**
- Tap **General**
- Tap **Reset**

Wiping your iPad pro contents
- Launch **Settings**
- Tap **General**
- Tap **Reset**
- Enter your passcode or Apple ID password if asked
- Now, tap **Erase All Contents and Settings**

Wiping your iPad pro via a Computer
- Connect **iPad pro** to your **computer** via USB cable
- From your Mac, click **General** at screen top. Click **Restore iPad**
- If you have a windows PC, launch **iTunes.** Next, from top left of iTunes, click the **iPad pro button**
- Click **Summary.**
- Click **Restore iPad**
- Obey instructions to complete wipe